The Happy Contractor

Acknowledgements

Thanks to John for the faith, patience and the logo design

Thanks to Janine and Sam for the encouragement and advice

The Happy Contractor

Rejecting traditional employment for the
freedom of contracting, and how to transition
successfully.

Alison Parfitt

The Happy Contractor by Alison Parfitt

Published by Parfenon Limited

© 2018 Parfenon Limited

www.parfenon.co.uk

Paperback ISBN: 978-1-9999949-1-4

Second Edition, May 2018.

Parfenon logo by www.pickleartuk.co.uk

Cover design by J. Dixon-Smith.

Contents

Introduction

If you're reading this book, there's a good chance you're wondering whether contracting is for you, and whether you could do it. This already puts you in a category of people with the open and enterprising mind-set suited to being a Contractor. If you've chosen this book you're probably a permanent employee wondering if there's another way to earn an excellent living without being chained to inflexible working arrangements, long hours and the daily grind. Perhaps you're searching for a way to be your own boss and a route to a freer life where you have more control over your work-life balance. Good for you.

Contracting in the context of this book describes professional people with a variety of different skill-sets and experience levels who have rejected the traditional employment model to take on short-term contracts with businesses in an industry setting, often paid by the day. Some people might also call them Consultants, as there are few differences. Others might use the term Freelancers, though whilst there are many similarities between Contractors and Freelancers, Freelancers are typically slightly different (the differences between these terms is explained later). The contracting market is diverse: executives, IT specialists, procurement managers and clerical staff are just a few examples. The advice in this book is aimed at would-be Contractors and Consultants and those just starting out, but much of it extends to aspiring Freelancers too, given the overlap. Seasoned Contractors and Consultants may find some parts helpful too.

I started contracting at the age of thirty, grateful for my work experiences up to that point, but eager to break free from the control employers had over my decisions, my personal life and the actual work I did. I wanted to earn a living in an autonomous way whilst maximising the financial return on my skill set and I was not prepared to wait for the wheel of career progression to turn whilst my best years passed by. I became frustrated with the monotony, the grind and the sluggish progression towards more dynamic working practices. With a background in commercial contracts (contract negotiation, contract management, tendering, procurement, commercial strategy) I knew my skills were in demand but had to take a leap of faith when transitioning because I didn't have a reliable source of all the information I needed, in one place, from someone who'd already done it.

Being female, and reasonably young, I was also an unusual demographic of Contractor. Contractors were always characterised to me as men who'd racked up many years of experience, or were at the end of their careers. But this is changing fast. There are significantly more women, and younger people, entering the contracting market.

So here it is, written down for you in as simple terms as possible, without lots of debate, unnecessary detail, or the history of one's life achievements. Contracting might feel like a big risk, or a leap into the unknown, but it doesn't have to be so daunting. This little book contains the key information you need to help you to:

- Understand how much work is out there for you and find work once you've made the transition
- Successfully transition from permanent employment to Contractor
- Set yourself up as a Contractor (with a simple checklist)
- Decide whether to trade as a limited company, via an umbrella company or as a sole trader and the differences between each
- Get to grips with how your money is extracted from a limited company should you choose to trade this way
- Pick a good umbrella company should you choose to trade this way

- Succeed at Contractor interviews and decide how much to charge clients
- Understand IR35 legislation and how to protect yourself against falling foul of it, in simple terms
- Understand the risks of being a Contractor and how to mitigate them
- Understand the role of your accountant
- Understand when you need to purchase Professional Indemnity insurance

And so that you can be sure contracting is the right decision for you, this book also gives you an honest account of:

- The benefits of being a Contractor
- What life is like as a Contractor
- How you might be treated differently as a Contractor
- Behaviours which make for happy clients
- Behaviours which are unproductive

Perhaps you're reading this on your daily

commute, your lunch hour, or with your last bit of energy after a long day. Perhaps you're feeling stressed out and undervalued, or you're just generally interested in how contracting might work for you as another way to live and to work. Perhaps you'd like additional income to invest in property, your pastimes, or your business venture ideas.

Contracting is not for everyone. The perceived or actual safety net of permanent employment is an absolute must for many, and understandably so. You may already know of Contractors who are making a success out of it, but perhaps you are wary of the risks. Nevertheless, if you would value more autonomy, more freedom, more time in which to live your life, variety and flexibility as well as excellent financial remuneration, then that old adage has never been truer: Fortune favours the brave.

And you don't even have to be that brave. Not if you're sensible, you plan for the change, minimise your risks and, of course, prepare yourself by reading this book.

Part 1

The Basics

1.1 Self-employed workers and the Contractor market

There were 4.8 million self-employed people in the UK in 2017 according to the Office for National Statistics,[1] and the growth of self-employment was one of the 'defining characteristics of the UK's economic recovery'.[2] The level of self-employment keeps on rising, with more people opting to be their own boss and work independently than ever before. Of these 4.8 million self-employed, roughly 2 million are Freelancers[3] (or Contractors, Consultants or whatever term describes short-term or project-based professionals) according to a report published by the Association of Independent Professionals and the Self-Employed (IPSE) in 2017.

As our economy changes, the traditional employment model is becoming outdated. Jobs for life don't really exist anymore and the generous final-salary pension schemes of decades past are effectively relics of this same historic era. People are starting second and third careers and working to an older age. And crucially, as humans, people are seeking more independence to get the most out of their lives.

In the UK, independent workers (i.e. those self-employed though choice) report being happier than traditionally employed workers, and many of the latter aspire to work in an independent way,[4] according to a report from McKinsey Global Institute in 2016. And it's not just workers with years of experience under their belts who are Contractors. IPSE also reported significant growth amongst younger Freelancers, with a 66% increase in Freelancers aged 16-29 between 2008 and 2016.[5] Further, IPSE found there are increasing numbers of women taking advantage of the flexible lifestyle freelancing offers, with a 55% increase in female Freelancers between

2008 and 2016 so that in 2016, women accounted for 41% of all Freelancers.[6] It's no longer an older male dominated landscape.

Contracting as a potential route is now on the radar of many graduates given that contracting is possible in such a wide variety of professions, skill sets and experience levels. There are some excellent potential benefits for workers only a few years out of university. Taking short-term contracts offers a fantastic way to gain a breadth of experiences, see the inside of different organisations and test different ways of working. It's a viable route to building a strong CV for future career progression. You just need to have skills businesses are interested in utilising flexibly over a shorter term, to fill a recruitment gap or an urgent need. And given the business benefits of buying in skills in a flexible way over the short-term, opportunities for younger Contractors will surely multiply.

1.2 Terminology: Contractors, Consultants and

Freelancers

Before going any further it's worth talking about the various terms which are often used interchangeably to describe short-term, temporary or project-based professional resource. The most common terms—Contractor, Consultant and Freelancer—overlap significantly, and there is no official definition of any. All three terms come under the umbrella of 'self-employed', and the typical features of each are as follows:

Contractor

Generally speaking, the term Contractor is used to describe a self-employed person who takes on short-term contracts which usually start at 3 to 6 months in duration but which are, more often than not, extended to last between 1 and 2 years. They contract with businesses or public sector organisations and usually trade through their own limited company or via an umbrella company (section 3.1 gives further explanation on these). They are usually paid a day rate or, less commonly, a fee linked to project milestones or project completion. Some Contractors are paid an hourly rate, and hourly rate contracts are sometimes paid less well. Often Contractors work for one client at a time, but not always.

Consultant: Consultancy Firms

Contracting and Consulting are terms which overlap greatly. Large firms (McKinsey, Deloitte, Ernst & Young to name a few) and other smaller consultancy firms typically go into large public and private sector organisations to work on specific improvement projects, providing advice and change recommendations which they may or may not assist in the implementation of. They are consultancy firms that provide organisations with Consultants, who are either their own employees, or associates. Associates usually work exclusively for the consultancy firm, are badged as such in front of the client, but are still self-employed and receive a day rate from the consultancy firm.

Consultant: Individuals

There are also individual Contractors who refer to themselves as Consultants. Fundamentally the same as Contractors, these Consultants will go into organisations to assist with specific projects or to provide expertise which may be lacking in the organisation. However, they normally possess a high level of expertise. The more skilled and experienced the Contractor, the more likely they will be to refer to themselves as Consultant, especially if they can command a high day rate. Individual Consultants are more likely to take on short-term contracts with multiple clients at the same time. They may or may not be involved in the implementation of the advice they provide to organisations and will often work at the client's office, as clients are likely to prefer them to be visible.

Freelancer

Freelancer and Contractor are often used interchangeably, but commonly Freelancer describes self-employed people who work with multiple clients at the same time, which can be both businesses and consumers. They are more likely to be home based or based at their own office, rather than working regularly from a client's office. There are many Freelancers in the media and creative industries (e.g. photographers, writers) but they exist in almost every industry and profession. Many people now freelance as a secondary income, and Freelancers are more likely to trade as a sole trader.

Whether you call yourself a Contractor, Consultant or Freelancer will depend on your skills, your clients, your industry, and the contracts you sign. There are no rules on what you call yourself. For example in the public sector, self-employed professionals are often referred to by civil servants as 'Contractors' regardless of their skills, experience or what they might have marketed themselves as. You don't even need to use any of these terms if you don't wish to: call yourself an IT Professional, Commercial Specialist, Interim Manager or some other preferred term if you like. Terminology does matter, but not as much as your actual skills and experience.

For the remainder of this book, I'll mostly stick with the term Contractor.

1.3 Permanent employment vs contracting

Getting out of permanent employment and becoming a Contractor means you'll trade away some of the comforts that you'll probably be very used to such as:

- sick pay
- holiday pay
- employer pension contributions
- the protection of a longer notice period (typically at least 4 weeks)
- redundancy rights you may have accrued
- a regular salary
- funded training courses
- employee benefit schemes (e.g. private health insurance, high street vouchers, car allowance etc.)
- access to resources like career advisors, occupational health, counselling services

Yet whilst you will give up these benefits you should expect to get the following in return as a Contractor:

- far greater autonomy over your work-life balance
- more freedom to choose when you take holidays (and for how long)
- power to make decisions about your working hours and working practices
- freedom to choose which projects to take on and to choose when to move on to the next one
- liberation from feeling controlled by an organisation or supervisory figure
- excellent financial rewards, with an income of around 50-100% more than salaried employment
- variety and breadth in your work
- an escape from corporate politics
- a way of giving yourself the breathing space to spend more time on hobbies, interests or even set yourself up to change careers

Think about your current situation and whether the potential benefits look attractive against what you'd be giving up. The reshuffle will not be for everyone, and rightly so. The "I don't want the stress of looking for work", or "I like knowing when my money is coming" type of worries are totally understandable...and can kill the idea of becoming a Contractor before you can say 'Professional Indemnity insurance'. If you are still interested, your appetite for uncertainty and risk will probably be a bit higher than many, and you'll be eager for change. The benefits and risks are explored in more detail in Part 4 of this book.

---

[1] Office for National Statistics (ONS), UK labour market: Mar 2017. *Estimates of employment, unemployment, economic inactivity and other employment-related statistics for the UK*, 15th March 2017, section 4.

[2] Office for National Statistics (ONS), *Trends in self-employment in the UK: 2001 to 2015*, 13th July 2016, section 1.

[3] Kayte Jenkins, *Exploring the UK Freelance Workforce in 2016*, IPSE: February 2017, page 2.

[4] McKinsey Global Institute, *Independent Work: Choice, Necessity, and the Gig Economy*, McKinsey&Company, October 2016, pages 53, 123.

[5] Kayte Jenkins, *Exploring the UK Freelance Workforce in 2016*, IPSE: February 2017 (IPSE), page 6.

[6] Kayte Jenkins, *Exploring the UK Freelance Workforce in 2016*, IPSE: February 2017 (IPSE), page 5.

Part 2

Finding Work

2.1 Is there enough work for you in your profession?

It is common for certain professions/role types to be more prevalent in the contracting market. One of the biggest is IT contracting in the UK, as it is often associated with short-term projects. There are also lots of contract roles which come into existence not for a specific project but to provide short-term support (e.g. 6 months to 2 years) to a business during a peak in activity, to fill a temporary recruitment gap, or simply to provide missing skills or resources in a flexible way. Examples of common professions or skill sets where contracting or freelancing opportunities exist are:

- IT / Software development
- Project Management

- Commercial/Procurement
- Accounting/Finance
- Engineering
- HR
- Senior Executives / Directors
- Administrative/Clerical/Payroll
- Training & Coaching
- Education
- Health/Wellbeing
- Creative/Media

The rise of self-employment and freelancing is testament to the fact that opportunities exist everywhere, and in its 2017 report IPSE found freelancers are present across all occupations.[7]

2.2 The search for work

The process of scoping out work opportunities can happen right away and there's nothing to lose in looking. Start having meetings or calls with recruitment agents before you hand in your notice in your permanent role and mine them for information. Try to find recruitment agents who deal with positions for someone of your skill set;

for example some agents specialise in the defence industry, or financial services. An excellent specialist recruitment agency for commercial and contract professionals is Arguile Search for instance, which typifies what you want and need in a recruitment agency: proactivity, attention to detail, integrity and frequent communication with candidates and clients. Many recruitment agents deal with all sorts of sectors and industries. Ask them questions like:

- How many Contractors do you see with a similar skill set?
- How often do contract positions come up for someone with my skill set? (Note that some agents will, for instance, specialise in finance and never deal with engineering.)
- When are the best times to look for work? (January and September are normally favourable.)
- What are the typical day rates for a Contractor of my skills and experience?
- Do you have any contract roles in the pipeline which might match my skill set?

- Which companies commonly use Contractors?

Don't be disheartened if you get some negative responses to these questions from recruitment agents. Each agent only sees a section of the whole market, so spread your net wide and speak to a large handful of agents. Don't put effort into maintaining relationships with the unhelpful ones, and maintain regular communication with the good ones—meeting face to face is best if possible. From these conversations you can scope out potential opportunities, and slowly get a feel for what work is available for your skill set. Whilst the best source of contract jobs is usually agents, as they often know of opportunities before they're even advertised, you can still pick up contract roles advertised on the big job sites if you put the effort into looking (i.e. don't just upload your CV and hope for the best).

Here are some examples of what I believe are the good ones:

- LinkedIn
- Jobsite
- Monster
- Total Jobs
- Indeed
- Security Cleared Jobs

A good agent can be extremely useful in helping you line up your first contract. If you have a short notice period in your permanent role, you might be able to line up your first contract before you've even handed your notice in. However, most people will have a longer notice period (at least 4 weeks) which will necessitate resigning before securing work as a Contractor. Slightly scary, but be brave. Just make sure that when you make the transition from permanent to Contractor, you have a financial buffer (see section 4.2.2 on this) so that you can avoid searching for work when you're in a weak financial position. Prepare yourself for the transition and do your research. Delay your transition to Contractor if you're overstretched financially.

2.3 Getting the best out of recruitment agencies

As a Contractor, reliable recruitment agency contacts are invaluable; the good ones do the sift work for you, which can save you trawling the job adverts online. Often agency contacts will know of roles which are coming up long before any job advert gets posted, and some roles will never even have a job advert posted on the big recruitment websites. Interesting roles in small companies may also come through agencies rather than being posted on job sites.

Many agencies make their money by charging a percentage or fixed fee on top of your day rate. Others might simply charge the client a finder's fee and then step out of the contracting chain— so your limited company or your umbrella company would contract directly with the client. Some agents might have agreed a rate with the client and might therefore try to squash your rate as low as possible.

If you build a good long-term relationship with your agency contacts, who will come to understand your skills and strengths, they can positively recommend you for positions over other potential contenders. They should also give you some insightful advice on what to expect for your interview.

Keep in regular communication with your agency contacts, keep them updated as to your availability and current contract end dates well in advance of the end of each contract (at least 3 months). Send them updated versions of your CV whenever you change contracts and remember that they are a valuable part of your network; you might end up knowing them for years.

2.4 CV tips

Contractor CVs contain much the same information as CVs for the permanent market, but they tend to be presented slightly differently. The first page of the CV should make it easy for the reader to see your relevant skills and experience.

CV format can be a subjective topic, but generally Contractor CVs are impactful if they are set out like this:

- Name and contact details (telephone and email)
- Profile/Professional Summary (a few brief sentences selling your skills and background)
- Key Skills and Achievements (if you can tailor or reorder these depending on what contract you're going for, great)
- Work History (keep it punchy, bullet points are good)
- Education/Training (going back as far as GSCEs is rare)
- Interests (needs to be very brief)

I like to keep my CV at two pages, but some Contractors have CVs of up to four pages. Longer than four pages and you're risking it being binned unread. Ensure the font is unfussy and easy to read—something like Arial, Times New

Roman or Verdana—and make doubly sure there are no spelling or grammatical errors.

2.5 Interviews

Be prepared to do more interviews than you would as a permanent employee. But bear in mind the interviews for contract roles tend to be shorter, are more likely to be CV based rather than competency based, and are almost never in form of an assessment day or aptitude tests (as these are expensive). Often Contractor interviews simply involve a 'chat', with varying formality. One large public sector organisation sometimes hires Contractors without any interview at all.

Some key dos and don'ts:

Do

- make sure you're able to confidently discuss the skills and experiences on your CV.
- maintain a positive, can-do attitude—you are selling valuable services.
- research the company and be able to ask intelligent questions about it and what the

client needs.

- research the interviewer(s) if you can. See if you can find out about their style and approach. A good agent will be able to help.
- be friendly. Maintain open body language and eye contact.
- note any guidance from agents; they will want you to get on well.

Don't

- mention your fee. It's better for the decision to hire and negotiation of the fee to be separate. However, if asked directly about your fee, be able to confidently state your requirements.
- promise what you can't deliver, or lie.
- disparage previous clients or colleagues, or generally talk in an unprofessional way.

2.6 Building and maintaining your networks

As you will know if you've moved around jobs before, this automatically grows your network as you connect with more people (especially since the birth of websites like LinkedIn). Your network should grow a lot faster as a Contractor and, as time goes on, this provides additional potential avenues of work. It goes without saying, but try not to burn your bridges! It's a small world and you're likely to run into people more than once. You never know who you'll end up working with or for, so ensure you're professional and leave a positive impression.

During the switch between permanent work and becoming a Contractor, leaving your permanent employment role on friendly terms keeps the door open to work in the future. As a contract resource, you are especially attractive to previous employers in times of resource or skill shortages because you know the business, and they know you. If they contact you directly they can avoid agency fees altogether: you could happily plug that gap on contract rates to everyone's convenience. Though if you do return to a previous employer as a Contractor, ensure you are fully aware of IR35 (see section 3.6).

Many Contractors will have had contracts which

they did not enjoy or did not go as well as they'd have liked, or clients they did not relish working with. You can choose never to work with them again—that's the beauty of being your own boss. But ideally you'll want to avoid any negative reactions when your name is mentioned. Maintain professionalism throughout, then get on with your life.

2.7 Flexibility in working arrangements

As a Contractor it is common to take on short-term contracts which are paid on a day rate, usually starting at 3 to 6 months in duration, but which, more often than not, are extended. You may also find contracts where you can charge an hourly rate for the work you output, remotely or at a client's office, or a mixture of the two. You may be able to work both of these types of arrangements concurrently with separate clients. Often Contractors are brought in to work on specific short-term projects and once the project is complete, your contract will end.

The key here is flexibility and being open to

opportunities. Consider your own personal preferences and work these around client needs.

2.8 Your Fee

It feels both wonderful and strange at first to think that (within market tolerances) you decide how much you will get paid. You value what you are worth: consider yourself as a business setting its prices, and remember that temporary skilled resources are in demand. Commonly, the lower the rate, the more likely it is to be specified as hourly, and the higher rates will be day rates.

In the months before you leave your permanent role to become a Contractor you can research how much others are getting paid in order to settle on a daily or hourly rate range at a value appropriate to your skills and experience.

Recruitment agents are an excellent first port of call to get an initial view once they've seen your CV. Obviously the internet is also fantastic for this (Contractor job boards) but you'll also get a lot of useful information from talking to people who either are Contractors, or who know Contractors and are reliable sources of information. Rates vary a lot; they depend on your skill set, whether you're working in the public or private sector and, crucially, what you can reasonably sell your skills for. Keep in mind how much negotiation leverage you have (or don't have).

It's impossible to give a ballpark figure for what you might charge right now, because the most common day rates range anywhere between £200 and £700 and each Contractor will have their own unique mix of skills and experience. From my personal experience as a commercial professional, if you are on a salary of between £50,000 and £60,000 in your permanent role, you should look to charge between £400 and £550 per day initially. Note that rates also vary across sectors. If you wish to calculate what you would need to charge as a day rate to bring the same amount home as your permanent salary, you can use a Contractor calculator (see further reading and resources at the end of this book) but note you'd need to charge much more than this to provision for pension contributions, periods without pay and the general risk and effort of finding work.

Agents that approach you with opportunities will often have a range of day rates the client is willing to pay, but there is always room for negotiation. You need to make sure you don't sell yourself short, but also remember if your client feels they're paying over the odds, they might not want to renew your contract and it might be hard to live up to expectations. Consider valuable trades such as reducing your rate for a longer contract, or for increased flexibility in your working arrangements.

2.9 Security clearance

A brief note for those with a defence or security background and holding a valid security clearance. If you don't work in a role that requires security clearance for 12 months, your security clearance lapses. The higher your level of security clearance, the faster it is likely to lapse. Bear this in mind as a Contractor: if your security clearance has lapsed you may be at a disadvantage to applicants that hold current security clearances. Officially however, you should not be overlooked if you do not have a security clearance but need one for a role. For example the Ministry of Defence contracting procedures are supposed to make sure there is no competitive advantage in having prior security clearances.

---

[7] Kayte Jenkins, *Exploring the UK Freelance Workforce in 2016*, IPSE: February 2017 (IPSE), page 2.

Part 3

Setting up as a Contractor

Part 3 of this book describes, in as basic terms as possible, how to set yourself up as a Contractor. It doesn't take as long as you think. But it can seem daunting if you don't know the various tasks you need to tick off and decisions you need to make in order to be ready to work as a Contractor.

There's a simple checklist at the end to help.

3.1 Ways to trade as a Contractor

As a self-employed professional you'll trade either via a limited company, through an umbrella company or as a sole trader. I have always traded via a limited company, which I set up right at the beginning of my contracting career.

A brief description of each is as follows:

A <u>limited company</u> is a separate legal entity in the eyes of the law and HMRC. You would set this up and register it at Companies House, and be director, shareholder and employee of this company. A limited company has limited liability, which means you and your company are separate legal entities in the eyes of the law. Practically speaking this means your company's debts are not your debts and vice versa, so if your company goes bankrupt, your personal assets cannot be claimed to pay your company's debts (unless you've committed fraud); however any money you have put into your company could be lost in the event of bankruptcy.

Most Contractors with limited companies tend to register for VAT because they are likely to exceed the £85,000 turnover threshold where registering for VAT is mandated (see section 3.7 on VAT). Once you're VAT registered, it means you have to charge VAT on all of your fees, and you can claim VAT back on company purchases. Your limited company also has to pay corporation tax on your profits which is calculated and paid annually. At the time of writing this book, corporation tax is set at 19%.

Umbrella companies exist to provide a contracting mechanism for Contractors. You are an employee of the umbrella company and would sign a contract with them. The umbrella company contracts with the employment agency who then contracts with the client, or the umbrella company contracts directly with the client itself. These companies normally take a fee for administration services out of your day rate, therefore what fee you are charged directly affects your take-home pay. Traditionally, trading this way shelters Contractors from worries around IR35 legislation (see section 3.6 which explains IR35), because the taxation level is the same as if you are inside IR35. Be warned, some umbrella companies are less reputable than others; see section 3.3 on how to choose a good umbrella company.

Becoming a <u>sole trader</u> is a very popular way to start up a business in the UK, but is much less popular amongst Contractors. You and your business are the same legal entity in the eyes of the law and HMRC which means that your personal assets (e.g. your house) can be claimed to pay your business debts if your business goes bankrupt ('unlimited liability'). You don't have to register for VAT unless your turnover is above the £85,000 threshold; below this threshold you can register for VAT voluntarily. As a sole trader you must submit tax returns each year and you do not have to pay corporation tax.

3.2 Deciding how to trade

How to decide which is best for you? Below are the pros and cons of each.

LIMITED COMPANY

PROS

• **Your income is maximised**

As the director and shareholder of your limited company, the biggest and most compelling advantage is that you can take your income in the most tax-efficient way possible. Usually, profit is extracted from the business by way of a mixture of dividend payments and a small salary. Trading through a limited company also provides the opportunity to claim a wide range of expenses as business costs (e.g. travel and subsistence, mileage, annual company events, entertaining) and also allows for tax planning opportunities. There are various decisions you can make with your accountant's advice about how and when to extract your profit from the business (e.g. the ratio of salary and dividend payments, when to take dividends to stay tax efficient, amount of pension contributions) but as a very rough rule of thumb, most Contractors working through a limited company can take home around 75-80% of their invoiced sums. So, if a contract was worth £80,000, you'd take home around £60,000 to £64,000 assuming your contract is outside of IR35. By way of comparison, take-home pay for a salary of £80,000 in a permanent role taxed via PAYE at 2018/2019 tax rates would be around £54,500 (before any pension or other deductions).

A brief explanation of how dividend tax works: dividends count towards your personal tax liability. For the 2018/2019 tax year the first £2,000 of dividends your receive are tax free. The next £32,500 received are taxed at 7.5%. However, as everyone has a tax-free personal allowance of £11,850, you can actually earn £46,350 (£11,850 + £34,500) before the tax rate on dividends rises to 32.5% (quite a dramatic increase in taxation). Remember though, if you are paying yourself a salary of £11,850 you'll start paying dividend tax at 32.5% on any dividends in excess of £34,500. Subject to any salary you may take, dividend tax rises again to 38.1% above £150,000. Each tax year your allowances are reset, so if you've drawn out a lot of dividends in one tax year, it can pay to wait until the next tax year before you draw out any more.

Dividend tax has gone up recently, but not enough to significantly change most limited company owner's profit extraction planning.

Accountants are the best source of advice on this, but you can find out more about dividends at www.gov.uk/tax-on-dividends.

•   Run your business like a business

Successful Contractors remember they are selling valuable services to other businesses or organisations. Offering your services through your own limited company adds credibility for potential clients. It is also exciting; you are running your own business after all. Design letterheads incorporating your company name, order professional business cards, create a company logo, register a domain and set up a website if you so choose. Who knows how your business might expand in the long term? An excellent example of such success is Commas Limited http://commas.biz. Based in Bristol, Commas was started as an individual consultancy and expanded successfully into supplying quality-assured commercial Contractors to organisations for short-term assignments.

CONS

- **Increased administrative burden**

You will need to ensure your company is set up and run properly and your affairs are in order, which includes ensuring that your accounts are submitted each year to Companies House, keeping company records, and reporting certain changes to Companies House (e.g. change of registered business address). You must also pay corporation tax, complete an annual tax return and file your company accounts once a year. To assist with this, most people employ an accountant, which provides you with assurance that everything's been done properly and you are compliant with tax legislation (see also section 3.5 on accountants). This greatly relieves but does not eliminate the administrative burden. That said, HMRC have made things much easier now that most of this can be done online. You will also need to arrange a company bank account which is separate to your personal bank account (see section 3.8 for more information on this).

- **Not as tax efficient for contracts which are inside IR35 legislation**

Most Contractors operate via their own limited company, but if you are working within the public sector, since the April 2017 'off-payroll' public sector legislation changes (see section 3.6.2 for an explanation of this), there is a much higher possibility your contract will be classed, by the public sector client, as inside IR35 legislation. In this circumstance, operating via an umbrella company might be a preferable option because being inside IR35 erodes the tax benefits of operating via a limited company. However, in the private sector—where the Contractor rather than the client still makes the determination on whether the contract falls inside or outside IR35—a limited company is the favoured option for Contractors. Keep an eye on what the government plans to do next with the 'off-payroll' changes, and see section 3.6.4 for more on how this piece of legislation might be expanded in the future.

UMBRELLA COMPANY

PROS

• **Small administration burden**

Trading through an umbrella company should result in the lowest amount of administration. As an employee of the umbrella company, you still have to be on top of your expenses (keep receipts for everything you can claim), and complete any required admin from them, but the company itself will deduct tax plus its administration charge, leaving you with little else to sort out. Because you are not a director of a limited company, you do not have the burden of additional statutory and legal duties, and you don't need to set up a separate business bank account. You will of course still need to purchase Professional Indemnity insurance, although sometimes this is included in the umbrella company's fee. See section 3.3 on how to choose a good umbrella company.

• **Easy to stop/start/change**

Trading through an umbrella company can be preferable for Contractors who may dip in and out of contracting, or those not sure how long they'll be contracting for. Compared with setting up a limited company it's much easier to enter and exit arrangements with an umbrella company. It is relatively easy to change your umbrella company each time you get a new contract, if you wish, or ditch the umbrella altogether should you decide to switch to one of the other forms of trading. However, changing umbrella companies in the middle of a contract is generally not a good idea because this creates an unnecessary administrative burden for the client (and yourself) with your contract having to be amended.

• No impact of IR35 legislation

By operating via an umbrella company, which will apply tax using the PAYE model, you are paying an equivalent amount of tax as though your contract was inside the IR35 legislation. Therefore, whilst you operate through an umbrella, you're not really at risk of falling foul of

IR35 (though it still pays to be aware of IR35 your status).

CONS

• **Reduced take-home pay**

As a rough rule of thumb, working through an umbrella company means you take home around 60-65% of your invoiced sums. So, if your contract was worth £80,000, you'd take home around £48,000 to £52,000, depending on the fee charged by the umbrella company. This is significantly less when compared to working through a limited company.

SOLE TRADER

PROS

• **Simpler tax affairs and administration**

Trading as a sole trader is a fast and simple way to start trading, but it's usually avoided by Contractors due to the reasons set out below. Your tax affairs are much more straightforward, you are not subject to much of the legislation of a limited company and you do not pay corporation tax. You need to do a tax self-assessment each year, which is relatively uncomplicated and done by many other self-employed people. Because of this you might only need an accountant's services once a year to assist with your self-assessment tax return (unless of course, you're comfortable doing this yourself). Trading as a sole trader is much more common for Freelancers, rather than Contractors.

CONS

• **Disliked by agencies and some clients**

If there is an agency in your contracting chain, the agent will usually insist Contractors operate via a limited or umbrella company in order to avoid responsibility, under tax legislation, for the correct income tax and National Insurance payments being made for the sole trader. This is one of the main reasons fewer Contractors tend to operate as a sole trader, as so many Contractor positions will involve contracting through an agent. Fears around sole traders accruing employment rights can also put clients off dealing with Contractors who operate as sole traders.

• **Not as tax efficient as a limited company**

You would pay income tax and Class 2 and Class 4 National Insurance on the taxable profits of your business, which is not as tax efficient as trading through a limited company. Take home pay is likely to be broadly equivalent to operating through an umbrella company.

• **Unlimited liability**

As a sole trader, you and your business are the same legal entity in the eyes of the law and this means that your personal assets could be used to pay the business debts in the event of bankruptcy.

3.3 Umbrella companies: how to choose

A good umbrella company should be swift to answer your questions, to process the timesheet you send in each week or month, and of course to pay you and provide your payslips. The only difference in take-home pay between umbrella companies is the level of fee you are charged for their services, because the taxation should always be the same (i.e. PAYE income tax and National Insurance).

Compare umbrella company fee structures and ensure you factor in any additional costs, e.g. entry and exit fees or blanket insurance cover which you might not need if you have already purchased Professional Indemnity insurance. A reasonable fixed fee usually proves much better value than fees which are set at a percentage of your income, which can become very expensive. Typical fees charged by umbrella companies can vary from £70 to £150 per month depending on your city and market rates.

When choosing an umbrella company, try to get a picture of how they treat their existing Contractor customers. For example, it's great if there is a direct dial to a specific member of staff (rather than having to call up through their public line, go through various options and then speak to someone different each time). Is there a guaranteed service level, e.g. response to queries within so many hours? Is there an online portal which will make submitting timesheets quick and easy?

Be careful of umbrella companies claiming very high retentions on income (e.g. "up to 85%"), as this is almost impossible to achieve whilst staying legal. For example, dodgy high retentions might sometimes be achieved through adding un-receipted expenses for meals which were never incurred. If HMRC were to investigate your tax affairs, you would need to be able to prove you had incurred the expenses you had claimed for; and if not, you'd bear the brunt of HMRC's wrath if caught out, not the umbrella company.

Agencies you deal with may have a list of umbrella companies they recommend, but you don't have to use these; the choice is yours. Here are some examples of what I think are decent umbrella companies:

- Cloud 9 Umbrella

(www.cloud9umbrella.com)

- Contractor Umbrella
  (www.contractorumbrella.com)
- Crystal Umbrella
  (www.crystalumbrella.com)

3.3.1 Health warning! Tax avoidance schemes

There are a number of Contractor tax avoidance or 'tax strategy' schemes in existence which, again, promote claims that you can retain very high percentages of your income (e.g. 80-90%). Often these involve an up-front fee paid by the Contractor and the scheme will probably involve some sort of loan arrangement. HMRC is coming down hard on the users of such controversial schemes, and many Contractors have experienced miserable, stressful times by becoming caught up in them. Whilst they might be tempting, it's much better to avoid them due to the havoc they can bring to your life if you find yourself under HMRC's microscope.

3.4 Insurance

Professional Indemnity insurance is a must,

regardless of how you choose to trade, and many clients will stipulate the need for Contractors to have this type of insurance within your contract. Professional Indemnity insurance provides cover for the cost of defending a claim from a client should they believe the service you have provided is unsatisfactory and has caused them to suffer losses. It's essential for peace of mind even if your contract doesn't specify you should have it, because even if you believe you haven't made a mistake, you might still be in a situation where you need to fight a claim.

You can expect to pay somewhere between £150 and £300 excluding Insurance Premium Tax (IPT) per year for Professional Indemnity insurance. A competitively priced, reputable insurance company is Larsen Howie www.larsenhowie.co.uk. Larsen Howie provides specialist insurance and IR35 advice to Contractors, Freelancers and Consultants and is certainly worth considering for your insurance needs.

You may decide to purchase other types of Contractor insurance, e.g. Public Liability, Jury Service etc., depending on the nature of your business. Some clients may specify you hold other types of insurance, e.g. some public sector bodies want you to have Public Liability insurance.

I have never had to claim on any of my Contractor insurance policies, and I do not know any Contractors who have had to either. Nevertheless, read each insurance policy thoroughly and take note of the exclusions. Take particular care not to invalidate the terms of your Professional Indemnity insurance; for example most policies will state you should not be signing contracts committing your client to contracts with third parties, or making business critical decisions. That is not to say that you cannot give business critical advice (you will of course wish to be as useful as possible) but the decision should not rest with you.

3.5 Accountants

Regardless of how you choose to trade, you'll want to ensure your tax affairs are properly conducted. If you choose to trade via a limited company where these will be more complicated, it is advisable to hire an accountant to help you, at least for the first few years. Getting things right when extracting your profit from a limited company is essential, as the money in your business bank account is not yours, it belongs to the company. Your accountant will advise you on how much profit is available in the business for payment into your personal bank account by way of dividends, and your corresponding personal tax liabilities.

Hiring an accountant will cost more than doing it all yourself of course, but it's worth it and it really takes the stress and worry out of things when you're starting up. Your accountant will sort your personal tax, VAT, company accounts and generally help keep you legal and organised with your business. That is not to say you don't need to put effort in yourself; you'll need to keep accurate records of your business costs, expenses, receipts, dividend payments, invoiced values etc. Often accountants will provide a simple spreadsheet or online portal for you to input your information, and you should keep the evidence (invoices, receipts etc.) in an organised way.

Many accountants now charge an all-inclusive fee of around £100 per month (ex. VAT) depending on which city you're in and market rates for accountants. If you're using a large accounting firm, make sure you get a dedicated person with a direct dial. Many accountants are sole traders, like my own accountant.

If you choose to trade as a sole trader or via an umbrella company, you'll need an accountant's services much less often, but it's a good idea to make contact with one and discuss when and how they'll support you (for example, it may just be assistance with your self-assessment tax return once a year, and occasional advice).

There are many accountants who are

experienced in supporting Contractors, and they don't even have to live nearby. I have never met my accountant, but we call and Skype where necessary. And pretty much all the paperwork is electronic. At the risk of labouring the point, if you choose to trade via a limited company and want to do your own accounting, you really need to make sure you know what you're doing.

3.6 Your tax affairs

If you choose to trade through a limited company (or as a sole trader) it's reasonably straightforward to ensure your day-to-day tax affairs are in order with the help of an accountant. If you choose to work through an umbrella company, it's even easier because your tax affairs are much simpler. And since IR35 only targets Contractors working through their own companies, it is not a concern for those working through umbrella companies because these Contractors are paying the equivalent amount of tax as if they were inside the IR35 legislation.

3.6.1 IR35: What is it, in a nutshell?

IR35 or the 'Intermediaries Legislation' is a piece

of tax legislation which came into force in April 2000 under the Finance Act. The reason it came into existence was to try to tackle 'disguised employment', which is a situation where a worker is contracted through their own company, instead of through an employment contract, but are essentially behaving and being treated like an employee. Situations were arising where an employee might resign or retire on a Friday and return on the Monday doing the same role, but as a Contractor. This effectively saved the employing organisation having to offer employment rights or benefits, and meant the worker paid less tax than an employee would.

Since the inception of IR35, this controversial piece of tax legislation has been criticised for its lack of clarity, poor design, deficient implementation, for damaging the self-employed economy and for victimising genuine Contractors who are contributing valuable skills to the economy in a flexible, short-term way. The criticism continues to this day. Historically, IR35 investigations are rare, and rarer still are the cases where HMRC has successfully proved a Contractor is a disguised employee and is therefore subject to IR35.

3.6.2 April 2017 'Off-Payroll' changes

Between the inception of IR35 in 2000 and April 2017, it was up to the Contractor (with the advice of their accountant or IR35 expert) to decide whether each contract they worked was inside or outside the IR35 regulations. If inside, they would pay tax in the same way as an employee (i.e. PAYE) and if outside, they could choose to take their earnings in a more tax-efficient way (e.g. a mixture of salary and dividends), as a business does. It was therefore the practice of Contractors to ensure their working practices and contract put them firmly outside the IR35 legislation; they tried to ensure they were not 'disguised employees'.

In April 2017, the government brought in 'off-payroll' changes to IR35 legislation, which affected Contractors working in the public sector. It took the responsibility for determining IR35 status away from Contractors, and forced public sector bodies to be responsible for determining the IR35 status of each Contractor working for it. Contractors working in the private sector were unaffected. The knock-on effect of the 'off-payroll' changes in the public sector was that public sector bodies generally took a risk-averse approach (often for fear of getting it wrong and being fined) and classed most Contractors working for them as being within IR35. As such, since April 2017, Contractors who remain working in the public sector usually work through an umbrella company (or through a larger consultancy firm), rather than through their own limited company. And this means that if you work in the public sector as a Contractor, you'll likely be paying more tax. However, it appears that the market is responding to this with day rates in the public sector rising in order to ensure Contractors are still encouraged to take up contract roles. Hence one of the reasons the 'off-payroll' changes were also heavily criticised.

At the same time as the 'off-payroll' rules were implemented, HMRC launched its CEST (Check Employment Status for Tax) online tool which is a questionnaire designed to determine a Contractor's IR35 status. The CEST tool has received criticism as it sets the bar very high for IR35 compliance and uses digital logic rather than a considered opinion based on case law. Many remain unconvinced of its helpfulness for Contractors, and do not see any incentive to use the tool unless they have to.

3.6.3 Protection from IR35

Many Contractors still favour trading through their own limited company, operating as a genuine business. Successful Contractors trading like this are aware of IR35 and protect themselves against falling foul of it. If you decide to trade this way, protect yourself by doing the following:

(i) IR35 contract review

Before you sign a contract, get it IR35-checked by a specialist. The specialist will review whether the wording of the contract puts it at risk of falling within IR35 legislation. If your contract has some risky clauses in it, the specialist will advise you on what changes to request with the client. Many clients are already very aware of IR35 and will have tried to make their contracts 'IR35 friendly'. Nevertheless, it's always worth getting a specialist review of your contract. Key aspects which will be checked in the IR35 contract review will include:

- Control. Would you be under the direct control and supervision of the client? If the contract clauses state this, or lean towards this, there is a strong chance the contract could be found to be within IR35.
- Substitution. Would you be allowed to provide a replacement to take your place to carry out the contract obligations? If the answer is clearly no, this is in dangerous territory with regards to being found to be inside of IR35.
- Mutuality of obligation. Does your contract say you are entitled to ongoing work or state

you are obligated to take additional work issued by the client? If so, this is also shaky ground for IR35 because this might leave you looking like an employee.

Note: make sure your working practices reflect what's in your contract, otherwise an IR35 compliant contract might not give you any protection. Another great source of information, specialist insurance services and advice for Contractors is Qdos Contractor. If you have purchased your Professional Indemnity insurance from Qdos Contractor they will normally review your contracts for IR35 for free. Alternatively, you can pay a fee to have your contract reviewed (often around £50 plus VAT).

(ii) Working practices
Once on contract, you should ensure you demonstrate working practices which put you outside of IR35. Your working practices should show you are working as a self-employed person rather than an employee. Practical things you can do to demonstrate this are:

- Use your own equipment (e.g. laptop, phone) if you can.
- Work from home sometimes.
- Politely and courteously tell your client when you will be taking time off for holidays/dentist etc., don't ask for approval like an employee would.
- Have your own company email address and use this when on contract if you can. If you have to use the client's email address ensure your email signature identifies you as an independent Contractor/Consultant.
- If you have business cards, make sure they show your company name, not your client's name.
- Vary your hours, don't work regular hours which are the same as employees'.
- Set up a website for your company and its services.
- Take opportunities to work for more than one client at the same time, if you can.
- Rectify errors in your own time and at your

own expense.

- Raise your own invoices under your own company-headed paper.
- Ensure you do not attend funded company functions like the Christmas party. If you do go, pay for yourself.

Keep proof that you've demonstrated the above as you go. You can even agree a 'schedule of working practices' with a client before starting work. If the client is happy to do this, it's a good way to protect yourself further.

(iii) Line up your support network

In the rare event of having to undergo an IR35 investigation, there are professional bodies who will step in to represent you in front of HMRC. Become a member and they will take the lead in representing you free of charge should you have to go through an IR35 investigation. For your annual subscription you also get a raft of other benefits such as compensation should your agency or client go bankrupt, should you have to attend jury service, should you become ill or injured or have to attend tax compliance meetings. One of the best is IPSE (Independent Professionals and the Self Employed) www.ipse.co.uk. Yearly membership costs are in the region of £176-£266 plus VAT. It's worth it.

Alternatively, or additionally, you can purchase Tax Investigation and Tax Liability insurance, to cover you for the cost of a tax investigation and any additional tax you might have to pay should you lose. This type of insurance also provides you with a dedicated professional who would take the lead to represent you in any tax investigation. Costs for this insurance start from around £100 (plus VAT) depending on your own personal circumstances and whether you want cover for a tax investigation only or tax investigation plus any additional tax liabilities, if you lose your case.

You may find yourself in one of the following situations:

- Your proposed contract wording puts your

contract role within IR35 and your client/agency refuses to amend it.

- Your client wants you to work in a way which places you inside IR35.
- Your contract tasks/objectives necessitate working in a way which puts you inside IR35.

In this event, consider working through an umbrella company and try to negotiate a higher day rate to compensate you for the loss of earnings. There are still some advantages to working a contract which comes inside IR35 through your limited company, simply speak to your accountant to decide on whether it's worth it. Lastly, if the contract and working arrangements look too unusual or risky or the client is too difficult, cut your losses and look for something else. That's the beauty of being a Contractor; if you don't want to work for an organisation, you don't have to.

3.6.4 Future IR35 changes and the contracting market

In the Autumn 2017 budget, the government

proposed applying the 'off-payroll' legislation to the private sector too, which would, in theory, mean private sector clients would be responsible for determining a Contractor's IR35 status. Many Contractor groups and accountancy firms suspect it is not a matter of if, but rather when, and bets are being placed on a 2019 roll out. The government is now in the process of consulting industry experts on this potential application of the 'off-payroll' changes to the private sector. Whilst many fear this will have a detrimental effect on the Contractor market in the private sector, it's important to point out that the public sector reacted to the 'off-payroll' rules in a typically risk-averse way, by classing almost every Contractor as inside IR35. And there are still huge numbers of Contractors working in the public sector via umbrella companies, with shrewd Contractors negotiating a higher day rate to compensate them for lost earnings. The private sector is likely to adapt to any application of the 'off-payroll' changes in a much more astute way.

The Contractor market is going from strength to

strength, offering skilled and productive labour on demand to the UK economy and it doesn't show any signs of slowing. What is the likelihood if 'off-payroll' is applied to the private sector? That the market will adapt, as it has done in the 18 years since IR35 came into force, and the Contractor market will continue to grow.

3.6.5 IR35 summary

Any quick browse on the internet on the subject of IR35 will reveal it's the subject of huge debate, consternation and fear amongst many. It's a serious subject, but there are some simple steps you can take to keep yourself compliant. The key is to keep abreast of any changes, pay your taxes on time, ensure your tax affairs are compliant, and protect yourself in the ways described above; then get on with your new life as a Contractor.

3.7 VAT

Most people know what Value Added Tax is because they pay it on goods and services they buy. At the time of writing this book, it is set at 20%. If you choose to operate as a limited company or a sole trader and your turnover is above £85,000, registration for VAT is mandated by the government. Below this threshold, you can voluntarily register for VAT. If you operate via an umbrella company, you do not need to register for VAT because you are an employee, not a business.

If you are VAT registered you must charge VAT on your services. Businesses which sell goods and are VAT registered charge VAT on the goods they sell, except for goods which are zero rated like children's clothes, books, newspapers etc.

If you are VAT registered as a Contractor and are billing a client £600 for example, you would add an additional 20% on top and show this in your invoice. The total sum due to you from the client would therefore be £720.

A VAT return, which calculates how much VAT you need to pay to the government, is prepared each quarter or year, normally by your accountant. Subtracted from this amount is any VAT you are entitled to reclaim for business-related goods or services (e.g. on office equipment like laptops or desk chairs). This is why VAT receipts are kept.

Usually Contractors will be on the flat-rate scheme where a fixed rate of VAT is paid to HMRC, or the cash accounting scheme where you pay VAT on your sales only when your customers have paid you. Take your accountant's advice on which scheme is most advantageous to you depending on your particular business circumstances.

Even if you suspect your turnover will be above £85,000 when you set up your company, you don't have to register for VAT right away, you can wait a few months and discuss the best course of action with your accountant. Being VAT registered is generally a must for full-time Contractors, who will normally exceed the £85,000 threshold. If you use an accountant, or even if you do it yourself, it's a relatively painless process and claiming back VAT can be an incentive if you intend to purchase office or computer equipment. Being VAT registered can also help to give your business a professional feel.

3.8 Setting up: checklist

Boiled down to a simple checklist, here's what you need to do in order to be ready to trade as a Contractor:

✓ **Decide how you're going to trade.**

(either as a limited company, via an umbrella company or as a sole trader).

If the answer is limited company then you need to do the following:

✓ **Set up your limited company.**

To set up my limited company I used A1 Company Services: www.a1companies.com. But there are many company formation services to choose from; just make sure they are above board and legitimate. All you need to do is check the availability of your chosen company name, complete a small amount of admin online and pay a small fee (around £30). Many Contractors will have simply been using their own name which then becomes Jo Bloggs Consulting

Limited. However, think carefully about whether you want to use your actual name. Why not pick something more interesting?

✓ **Set up a business bank account, in your company's name.**

I went with Natwest Business, because Natwest (at the time) were offering 2 years' worth of free business banking. I now pay a charge of £5/month to Natwest for banking services. This is fairly typical.

Or if you choose to trade via an umbrella company you'll need to:

✓ **Make sure you choose a reputable umbrella company.**

You'll need to complete some forms for the umbrella company and give them some details, but this should be a relatively painless process.

Or if you choose to trade as a sole trader you'll need to:

✓ **Crucially: ensure your client is happy contracting with a sole trader.**

If so, you just need to start recording your costs and expenses ready for your self-assessment tax return.

And regardless of how you choose to trade you also will need to:

✓ **Choose and employ an accountant.**

As mentioned in section 3.5, if you are running a limited company, it's likely you'll need to agree to a monthly arrangement with an accountant. If you choose to trade as a sole trader or via an umbrella company, you'll need an accountant's services far less.

✓ **Purchase a Professional Indemnity insurance policy.**

Regardless of how you choose to trade, as a Contractor you'll always need Professional Indemnity insurance. I get mine from Qdos Contractor (see section 3.4).

Part 4

Is it Right for Me?

What is life really like as a Contractor and what is the benefit and risk package when compared to the perceived safety of permanent employment? In this section, I'll try to set this out with the end goal of helping you decide whether contracting is for you, with as much honesty about the downsides as enthusiasm about the upsides. I have done my utmost to ensure that the descriptions of the benefits are not overblown and likewise the risks are not trivialised, but we all know experience is subjective. You might decide it's for you now. You might decide it's not. You might decide it's not for you now, but in five years you'll give it a shot (if this is really your conclusion, just don't let it become one of those things you always say you'll do, but never get round to).

4.1 The benefits

If you are considering contracting, you probably already have a view on what the benefits are, and how valuable these benefits would be to you personally. Clearly for many people, a permanent job with a pension scheme, relative job security and a reasonable salary is comfortable and a change to this status quo is unattractive for a whole variety of reasons. Fair enough; don't become a Contractor. However, given you're reading this, this probably doesn't describe you. So, without over-amplifying them, here are the benefits:

4.1.1 Autonomy over your work-life balance and freedom to decide when to take time off

Becoming a Contractor is a change in mind-set, and it is a change in lifestyle if you want it to be. You decide how much you are paid (within market tolerances), your working pattern, and when you take holidays. The more hours you put in, the more you get paid, which, for me, felt wonderful after sinking so many evenings and weekends into my permanent roles and feeling rather burnt out (and slightly resentful) after a while. The taking back of control of your time, your holidays and your working pattern can feel extremely liberating and can seriously enrich your work-life balance. I have a Contractor friend who regularly takes 2-3 month breaks between his contracts to invest in his woodwork hobby. Others maintain a comfortable lifestyle whilst only needing to work part-time as a Contractor. I can relate to this, as I have also in the past decided to take a part-time contract in order to focus on other business ventures and my creative pursuits, which would have been impossible for me when working in a busy permanent role.

Another great example of Contractors having additional scope to spend time on other business ideas is www.SmallOutside.com. A promising start-up which offers high-quality IT services to organisations via an innovative crowd consulting model, SmallOutside.com was launched by another Contractor friend who was able to provision sufficient funds and set aside a whole year to dedicate to this business venture;

something he acknowledges would have been impossible had he continued in this permanent job.

Many other Contractors that I have known have sought to maximise their income by lining up their contracts back-to-back, working full-time and taking next to no holidays thus strengthening their financial position for a very early retirement or to fund other business ventures. Do all of the above when it suits you, if you want. Crucially, the choice is yours.

4.1.2 Financial rewards

Organisations in the public and private sectors buy in Contractor skills on a short-term basis without the burden of having to employ them and give them all of the employment rights and benefits due to permanent employees. Clearly this is extremely convenient for businesses and public sector organisations, either in times of rapid growth, flux or where it is not in the business interest or strategy to add more staff to headcount figures. For them, it can be a cost-effective way of ensuring the right skills and resources are in place on a temporary basis. Because Contractors swap out the rights and benefits of permanent employees, have to build a stable financial position to allow for potential periods without work and during times of sickness and holidays, fund their own pension, and put effort into securing their own work opportunities, it is an economic necessity that Contractors need to be paid significantly more than permanent staff. In business, with risk comes reward. This is why you should expect to earn 50-100% more as a Contractor than you would as a permanent member of staff. Consider that contracting offers a route to maximising your skills and experience for the best possible financial return. How you determine your fees is explored in section 2.8.

4.1.3 Variety in your work

Sometimes it can be hard, or take a long time, in a permanent role to experience a good breadth in your work, experience a number of roles, organisations, or industries. Permanent employees run a higher risk of getting stuck in a role, or perhaps being moved onto a project they're not keen on, and they will have differing levels of influence over what they work on. As a Contractor, you can expect involvement with a variety of different projects over shorter time periods. This can be hugely beneficial to your CV. You might even find it easier to get roles in different industries, further adding strings to your bow (which has been my experience). It will also positively affect your personal development; it's a real breath of fresh air when you work with someone who's moved around lots of organisations and experienced lots of different working environments, rather than being institutionalised within one big organisation.

4.1.4 Freedom to choose which projects to take on and freedom to choose when to move on to the next one

Search for and agree to work on projects that interest you, and work for clients you like the look of; the power is in your hands. Not only can you seek out and take up the work that interests you, you can also walk away if you find it's not a good match for your skill set or career objectives. Whilst it's probably not a good idea to leave organisations in the lurch because you've got bored with the work they've given you, making a decision to leave for the right reasons in open dialogue with your client is unlikely to harm your future contract prospects. If you do happen to find a scarcity of work, you may have little or no choice in which contract you take up, but the critical thing is the decision power is in your hands and no one else's.

4.1.5 Leaving behind the corporate politics

Empire building, rivalries, workplace bitchiness, giving and having appraisals, dealing with staff issues, organisational change initiatives. Whilst a few of these add value to businesses, all of these things can distract from delivering value in a role, and can cause additional unwelcome stresses on top of the burden of performing well. Contractors are so much freer. What a relief it is not to have to take part in endless box-ticking appraisal activities. This is not to say you can't ask clients for constructive discussions about your performance! This can be really valuable. And if you find you're not keen on a certain someone, at least you only have to tolerate them for months, not years (or for as long as you feel like it).

4.1.6 Breathing space to pursue hobbies and interests, or even change careers (if you so choose)

During 2016/2017 there were 526,000 people suffering work-related stress, depression or anxiety,[8] according to the government's Health and Safety Executive. We are often warned that chronic stress has a devastating effect on our physical and mental health. Our life outside of work is critical in relieving work-related stress and as a Contractor you have additional scope to make sure you spend enough time with your loved ones or pursuing your outside interests, by engineering breaks between contracts, and working manageable hours. You have the potential to fit in more opportunities for exercise with flexible working practices, work from home more regularly, and reduce or avoid relentless exhausting late finishes in the office. If you do find yourself regularly in the office until 8pm, at least you're working late for the benefit of your own business, as well as your client's. And there's more chance you're being paid for the extra time you've put in.

The flexibility of contracting and the improved financial position can also give rise to opportunities to transition to a new career. For example, you can use breaks between contracts or take part-time work to put time and effort into a new venture, or a hobby that might one day be a new income stream. Part-time opportunities might be rarer, but they certainly exist. One of my most interesting contracts was part-time, working three days a week for one client whilst I did ad-hoc work for another client and wrote this book. After all, a business might not have enough work or the budget for a full-time Contractor, but it may still need your skills and experience some of the time.

4.2 The risks, and how to minimise them

Now for the potential downsides of becoming a Contractor. As you would imagine, these are primarily to do with the risks of finding work and loss of employment rights. There are real risks, but these downsides can be over-inflated when viewed from the comfort of a permanent role. Once you are a Contractor, you'll see the risks for what they are—manageable. And whilst the switch from permanent employee to Contractor can be scary, being concerned about the risks certainly doesn't mean contracting isn't for you. Here are the main risks and downsides, and how to get comfortable with them.

4.2.1 Uncertainty of getting work

Given the short-term nature of the contracting market, it's common to find it difficult to line up work more than a few weeks in advance. It is, therefore, very likely that you'll need to hand in your notice in your permanent job without having any contract work lined up (as I did). Nerve-racking stuff, but don't panic.

Before you leap, you can look. Prior to handing

in your notice for your permanent role, meet with agency contacts in your city to scope out how much contracting work there is for your skill set and experience. As mentioned in section 2.2, agents should be able to help paint a realistic picture of how easy it would be for you to find work. If you get a consistent message that there isn't any contracting work for your skill set, don't risk it—you've lost nothing in finding out. Or find a way to acquire the skills you need to become a Contractor in a related field.

Assuming you are getting some positive responses to your enquiries, try to make and maintain good relationships with three to five good agents, so your net is spread wide. Prime your agents with your CV and the date you are available to start work. The good agents are proactive and always want to add good professionals to their network.

You can do all of this groundwork before you hand in your notice—zero risk to you—ensuring you get a good feel for your contract employment prospects in your city or region and preparing the ground for your entry into the Contractor market. With a typical permanent role notice period, it's likely you'll still have to hand in your notice without a contract position lined up, but at least you'll have a good feel for the market, you'll have your agency network established, and be ready to trade as a contractor (as described in Part 3 of this book).

For Freelancers likely to deliver smaller projects for multiple clients, you could already be making the transition whilst working your permanent role—taking on small projects for clients which you could complete at the weekend or during evenings, assuming you have the time and your employment contract doesn't restrict you from doing this. Alternatively, reduce your hours in your permanent role in order to take on freelancing work, so that when you do finally hand in your notice, you'll already have a small client base to build on.

4.2.2 Financial risk

You'll need a contingency fund of course. Firstly, to cushion you for the transition to contracting, and then to keep aside for a rainy day if you find yourself in an unplanned break between contracts. Everyone's risk profile is different; how stretched you are with mortgage/rent or other debt payments, whether you have dependents to support, and whether you have the benefit of a partner's income all play into how much financial strain you'll feel under. Some Contractors are in their 50s and 60s by the time they start contracting and have the safety of a pension to rely on. When I started contracting, I was the main breadwinner, was in the middle of a house renovation and had a mortgage to pay. In hindsight, my contingency fund was lacking. It is sensible to make sure yours can cover you for at least three months without work. I don't know any Contractors who have been out of work for more than a couple of weeks other than by choice, so it's extremely unlikely you'll need it for this long. But at the very least it will protect your mental wellbeing, and with the benefit of a decent contingency fund you can focus on finding work without a sense of panic that might see you taking on contracts which you don't want, have to travel too far for, or which are not at an appropriate rate for you.

Once you've landed your first contract and you've banked a few good pay cheques, you're up and running and making a good income. From then on as you strengthen your financial position, gather contacts, add valuable history to your CV, and gain further knowledge of the market, the risks shrink. Continue to make sure you put enough aside to cover you for planned breaks in your earnings like holidays; maintaining a buffer of three months' income is a good amount to aim for. Clearly your ongoing contingency fund is also necessary in case of sickness, though some Contractors do purchase Income Protection insurance.

If you are already overstretched financially, or have health concerns, think carefully about whether you can tolerate the extra risk of being self-employed. Sick pay in a permanent role is a valuable safety net if you are seriously unwell.

4.2.3 Pensions

It's easy when an organisation takes care of your pension for you; your employer contributes and so do you. You don't really have to spend much time thinking about it or making a huge number of investment decisions.

As a Contractor, you need to fund your pension. However, if you are trading through a limited company, your company can make your pension payments and take advantage of significant tax incentives from the government. Despite missing out on contributions from an employer your earnings as a Contractor should provide ample scope to invest in a decent pension scheme. You can take full control of your pension via a Self-Invested Personal Pension (SIPP), or pay a financial adviser to manage your pension investments for you. Just make sure you make adequate arrangements to invest a chunk of money in your pension. You can do this each month, or as a lump sum each year. Some

Contractors don't even do this; they invest in property, or other business ventures, in place of traditional pension arrangements.

Many people stay put in organisations because of a generous pension scheme and in this changing world, this is totally understandable. I chose to leave a generous final-salary pension scheme to go my own way, and I don't regret it for a second.

4.2.4 Your ego, and the potential loss of status

Have you worked hard to acquire status, rank or power in an organisation? Most of us will have done, to varying degrees. Perhaps you are used to having direct reports, or even dedicated secretarial support? We all have egos to feed which are inextricably linked to how well we feel we're doing in our careers and our lives, and where one sits within a hierarchy might play heavily into this. Initially being an 'unknown' Contractor in an organisation and sitting outside of that organisation's hierarchy might therefore sit uncomfortably with your ego. This change of status or adjustment to how you are perceived by others is something to test yourself on before committing to life as a Contractor. That's not to say you are without status, rank or power as a Contractor. You are an independent expert, a business and a free agent which some of the permanent employees you work with (or varying positions) may well aspire to be one day.

On the same theme, and putting financial rewards aside, how will you feel if you're asked to deliver work which is clearly below you level of skills and expertise? This is likely to happen at some point and my advice would be to deliver such work without negative comment and with grace. If your skills are being drastically under-utilised or you're yawning and twiddling your thumbs (less likely in the private sector) you'll probably want to have a tactful discussion with the relevant decision maker within that organisation to discuss how best to ensure you're adding value. You could also choose to stay quiet and take the money in this unlikely situation, however beware; this course of action risks you becoming deskilled and eventual questions about what value you're providing to the client will be highly likely.

4.2.5 The successful mindset of a Contractor

Breaking out from permanent employment and running your own affairs offers more freedom. When you get up in the morning to go to work, you are doing it because you have chosen to. There's no employer to blame for the fact you're sat at a desk on a Monday morning when you wish you were still in bed. The amount of work you do correlates exactly to how much you earn, and this should provide excellent motivation. This self-starting mind-set is at the heart of being a successful Contractor, and it will translate into job satisfaction, mental wellbeing and financial prosperity. It's a wonderful feeling.

If this doesn't sound very you, and you need a boss or employer to provide you with the motivational 'stick' to make it in to work for 9am, consider carefully whether the Contractor life is for you.

4.3 Treatment as a Contractor

As a Contractor, you can and should expect to be treated differently in some ways, compared to how you used to be treated as a permanent employee, and compared to the permanent employees that you might be working with.

Will you enjoy being a Contractor, and will you be comfortable with the way you are treated as a Contractor? Going into and working within an organisation as a Contractor is different to starting in a new organisation and working as a permanent employee. Whilst it is common courtesy to be shown where the toilets, kitchen or shop are, don't expect to spend much time in any induction and orientation programme. Most clients will be looking for good value as soon as possible and will expect productive behaviours, so you'll need to try to hit the ground running.

As much as you will behave differently as a Contractor, you will be treated differently by many as a Contractor. The switch in behaviour between being a permanent employee and a Contractor might take some getting used to, and the experience can be both positive and negative. Clearly all organisations have their own cultures, full of unique individuals, and so experiences will of course vary. However, there do seem to be some common themes in the experiences of the Contractors I have known.

4.3.1 Public sector vs private sector

One common theme is the difference between working in the public sector and the private sector. In the public sector, Contractors (individual skilled professionals as well as big consulting firms) are providing essential support to many organisations which struggle to recruit and retain permanent staff with the desired skill set. In this respect, the public sector continues to be a rich source of contracts for Contractors. However, whilst taking contracts in the public sector is likely to add a valuable string to your bow and excellent breadth to your CV, the experience of working in this sector, particularly if you are not used to it, can prove challenging.

After working primarily in the private sector, I

found the excessive levels of bureaucracy hard to get used to. Decision making felt slow, or escalated to unnecessarily senior levels, and in general productivity levels in the wider organisation seemed to struggle when compared to the private sector. Nevertheless, it was an excellent experience for me, as I found myself in a crack team chosen for their abilities to get a job done under gruelling timescales with a mandate to succeed despite all of these challenges.

It also seems to be the case that a contract taken within the private sector is more likely to be better organised—there will be a pressing need, urgent tasks and projects with your name on them. Private sector companies cannot afford to hire expensive professional support and not utilise it properly, as I saw happen in the public sector. As such, some Contractors find working in the private sector can be more rewarding on a personal level than working in the public sector. That said, it can often be what you make of it; so if you put effort in to ensuring you add value, you are likely to be rewarded with a more valuable contract experience, as mentioned in section 4.2.4.

4.3.2 Being part of a team (or not)

Each role as a Contractor can take a different form. Sometimes you may be given tasks which involve little interaction with the client's employees. More commonly, you'll work with a team, or key individuals. Be prepared for a slower integration into a client's team environment, or none at all, compared to if you were a permanent employee. Your status is different, and to some, you might remain an outsider; you are not under the direct control of the client, and they do not have the same power over you. You are also only a temporary addition to the team, which may mean people put in less effort to include you. If you're working away from the client's premises regularly, this is more likely. Might this be too uncomfortable for you? More often though, the permanent employees you work with will be welcoming and delighted to have extra help.

4.3.3 Dealing with resentment

You may experience occasional resentment or friction from non-Contractor co-workers at some point during your contracting career. Friction can arise amongst clients' permanent staff for a number of reasons: they may feel you're telling them how to do their job; they may be upset that you're paid more or you might simply be an unwelcome outsider—a threat of sorts.

For example, there persisted a strong 'them and us' (Contractors and permanent staff) atmosphere at the public sector organisation I worked at which seemed to permeate many parts of it except for a few highly productive teams (one of which I was lucky enough to work in) and more senior staff members. Around the organisation, I often witnessed (and occasionally experienced) resentment towards Contractors, apparently mostly fuelled by the pay differential and a misunderstanding or ignorance of the different risk package Contractors accept. The fact that many Contractors provided essential help seemed immaterial to those feeling resentful. A small number of Contractors did appear to deliver little value, but were kept on despite this. This may well have contributed to feelings of ill will.

I've always preferred to work in an environment as harmonious as possible, and therefore have always done my best to avoid upsetting anyone. Sometimes though, just your presence can ruffle feathers and there's not much you can do about it. What you can do is be respectful and helpful when working with client personnel, and develop productive working relationships.

How challenging you find any negative reactions depends on your outlook and personality type; perhaps it won't bother you at all. At any rate, your Contractor skin will soon toughen.

4.4 Behaving as a Contractor

Once you've found your first contract role, prepare yourself for the shift in behaviour from permanent employee to Contractor. You are providing valuable short-term advice and skills to an organisation and you are independent and separate to that organisation. You have been brought in because you offer something that the company needs, there is an equitable relationship—but you are, at first, an unknown quantity. After some time in a permanent role, we all build up a reputation and our colleagues know us as hardworking and skilled individuals. Each time you work for a new client, you'll need to build a solid first impression. Friendliness, openness and approachability are key in developing good working relationships. Whilst being self-assured, avoid any hint of arrogance and try to employ tact and diplomacy and be as helpful as possible. If your client colleagues enjoy working with you, there's more likelihood of your contract being extended.

4.4.1 Minimising disruption

When you first start a contract, there will be a steep learning curve as you focus on getting yourself up to speed so you can add value as quickly as possible. Permanent employees would usually get various inductions and lots of objective-setting discussions, but as a Contractor it's unlikely you'll get this level of interaction; organisations will want to get as much out of you as possible without significant time investment in you.

Whilst we all want to hit the ground running at the start of a new contract, of course it will take a while to get your head round the job. Hopefully you'll have some sort of kick-off meeting with your client including one or some of your new colleagues, so make sure you get maximum value out of this. Come prepared with focused questions about what success looks like, what you are there to help with, who you should work closely with, where you can find information and so on. Be organised and try to proactively find the information you need without constantly interrupting people. Schedule weekly progress update meetings with your client and ask your questions then, and don't be scared to say 'I don't know' at first; just ensure you proactively find the answers. I worked with a Contractor for a couple of weeks who was very disorganised, late to meetings, couldn't manage their inbox ("I don't remember getting that email") or communicate clear progress to the client. Their communication style was teeth sucking and no can do and they routinely interrupted colleagues with low level, repetitive questions. Their contract was terminated before the end of the first three months. Basically aim for the opposite of this!

I worked with another Contractor who was constantly knocking on the office doors of the senior leadership team, asking to run ideas past them or chat things through. The Contractor was tactfully moved out of that office into another one, further away from the senior leadership team. Part of the role of a Contractor is effective communication with your client; you need to communicate success and progress but timing of the communication is also important. Politely ask when good times to talk are. Generally speaking people will be happy to help you and tolerant of questions. But be careful not to use up the goodwill you're afforded.

4.4.2 Useful behaviours

In order to add as much value as possible, your client colleagues should find it easy to approach you. As mentioned, friendliness and openness go a long way. So do tact, integrity, being professional and of course being productive. Deliver quality work. Look for ways to add value (but don't overstep). One Contractor I worked with made up their own tasks if they found themselves with a spare half hour; digging up 'problems' which they began communicating to senior staff members, causing all sorts of headaches for them. Tread carefully! You can create all manner of political problems if you begin defining your own work package when it's not welcome.

Try not to become defensive if you receive constructive criticism. What is it that your client needs you to do for them? This may be crystal clear, but if it's not, employ effective communication skills to get to the bottom of what you need to deliver. Above all, effective and appropriate communication (at the right times) will play heavily into how much you enjoy your contract, and how happy you make the client. Ensure you are delivering updates on your progress to the client at appropriate intervals. Ask for feedback and check the client is happy with your work.

4.4.3 Unproductive behaviours

As mentioned earlier, it can be challenging when you're used to having a good reputation in a company, built steadily and strongly over some years, to go into a new company as a temporary resource and start afresh. Capability is expected and you should be confident you can deliver value. But there's no need to go on about your various career achievements to your colleagues. One Contractor I knew felt the need to talk about their credentials and success stories repeatedly; this is unnecessary (you've already got the job!) and can seem pompous. Remain tactful at all times. Do not treat people like they're your secretaries. You have been brought in to help, and help you must. You should get your hands dirty, produce results and expect to have to pull your weight. Don't create unnecessary extra work for your colleagues by asking them to do what you haven't got time to do, unless it's been agreed and they are willing to help you. And obviously, talking about how much you earn as a Contractor or criticising your client's organisation are clearly unwise things to do.

---

[8] Health and Safety Executive (HSE), *Work-related Stress, Depression or Anxiety Statistics in Great Britain 2017*, November 2017, page 2.

Final thoughts

It's so easy to focus on the immediate challenges of the day or week, grind out your time at work and let the years roll on by. But if you're not content with your work arrangements, it doesn't have to be your life. Times are changing, and there has never been a better time to fulfil a desire to work for yourself, if you have the inclination.

Becoming a Contractor has changed my life for the better: given me a sense of freedom and autonomy, hugely benefitted my work-life balance, greatly reduced my stress levels and allowed me the time to explore other interests whilst maintaining a stronger financial position and a more comfortable lifestyle. There are real risks involved, but they are mitigable and do reduce in size over time.

Change can be scary, but you don't have to make the change before you're ready. And it's not a one-way street either; if it doesn't work out or you don't like it, you can get another permanent job. Try again in a few years.

Chances are, if you've read this book, you have an enterprising spirit and a slightly higher appetite for risk. You are also likely to seek out ways to do things differently in your life, with you at the helm.

Welcome to the club and I wish you the very best of luck with your contracting future.

Note from the Author

If you've enjoyed this book, would you consider rating and reviewing it please?

Thank you.

You can find out more about the author's business, Parfenon Limited, by going to www.parfenon.co.uk.

Further reading and resources

The focus of this book was to provide the key information, rather than an encyclopaedia, to the reader. There is a huge amount of information on the internet of varying quality. I have set out some good sources of additional information below:

- Setting up a limited company

Form your limited company via companies house www.gov.uk/limited-company-formation

Form your limited company through A1companies.com www.a1companies.com

- Umbrella companies

Contractor UK article on umbrella companies www.contractoruk.com/umbrella_company

- IR35 and new 'off-payroll' rules

IPSE's guide to IR35
www.ipse.co.uk/resource/guide-to-ir35-v1-pdf.html

Contractor Weekly IR35 guide
www.contractorweekly.com/ir35/ir35-guide/

- Insurance

Larsen Howie Website
www.larsenhowie.co.uk

Qdos Contractor Website
www.qdoscontractor.com/insurance

- Income calculators

www.contractorcalculator.co.uk/calculators.aspx

- Association of Independent Professionals and Self-Employed (IPSE)

www.ipse.co.uk

Bibliography

Health and Safety Executive (HSE), *Work-related Stress, Depression or Anxiety Statistics in Great Britain 2017*, November 2017. Retrieved from: http://www.hse.gov.uk/statistics/causdis/stress/stress.pdf

Kayte Jenkins, *Exploring the UK Freelance Workforce in 2016*, IPSE: February 2017 (IPSE). Retrieved from: https://www.ipse.co.uk/uploads/assets/uploaded/de84dfb7 -283a-4c26-ba446f95f5547c1f.pdf

McKinsey Global Institute, *Independent Work: Choice, Necessity, and the Gig Economy*, McKinsey&Company, October 2016. Retrieved from: https://www.mckinsey.com/~/media/McKinsey/Global Themes/Employment and Growth/Independent work Choice necessity and the gig economy/Independent-Work-Choice-necessity-and-the-gig-economy-Executive-Summary.ashx

Office for National Statistics (ONS), *Trends in self-employment in the UK: 2001 to 2015*, 13th July 2016. Retrieved from: https://www.ons.gov.uk/employmentandlabourmarket/peo

pleinwork/employmentandemployeetypes/articles/trendsi
nselfemploymentintheuk/2001to2015

Office for National Statistics (ONS), *UK labour market: Mar
2017: Estimates of employment, unemployment, economic
inactivity and other employment-related statistics for the
UK*, 15th March 2017. Retrieved from:
https://www.ons.gov.uk/employmentandlabourmarket/peo
pleinwork/employmentandemployeetypes/bulletins/uklab
ourmarket/mar2017

Go your own way.

Bristol based art, design and illustration
www.pickleartuk.co.uk

Commercial Consulting
www.parfenon.co.uk